#PARTNER tweet

140 Bite-Sized Ideas for Succeeding in Your Partnerships

By Chaitra Vedullapalli
Foreword by Dr. Petri Salonen

Copyright © 2010 by Chaitra Vedullapalli

All rights reserved. No patent liability is assumed with respect to the use of the information contained herein. Although every precaution has been taken in the preparation of this book, the publisher and author(s) assume no responsibility for errors or omissions. Neither is any liability assumed for damages resulting from the use of the information contained herein.

First Printing: March 2010

Paperback ISBN: 978-1-61699-012-1 (1-61699-012-0)

Place of Publication: Silicon Valley, California USA

Paperback Library of Congress Number: 2010922179

eBook ISBN: 978-1-61699-013-8 (1-61699-013-9)

Trademarks

All terms mentioned in this book that are known to be trademarks or service marks have been appropriately capitalized. Happy About® and its imprint, THINKaha™, cannot attest to the accuracy of this information. Use of a term in this book should not be regarded as affecting the validity of any trademark or service mark.

Warning and Disclaimer

Every effort has been made to make this book as complete and as accurate as possible, but no warranty of fitness is implied. The information provided is on an "as is" basis. The author(s) and the publisher shall have neither liability nor responsibility to any person or entity with respect to loss or damages arising from the information contained in this book.

Advance Praise

"Don't underestimate this book by its size; this compendium is packed with game-changing ideas on how to effectively transform customer relationships into strategic partnerships which are sure to drive sustainable value across every aspect of the business—and a read I would turn to time and time again."

Christopher Boucher, Senior Director, Customer Management IQ, International Quality & Productivity Center

---

"Short. To the point. Clear partnering advice. Now that's refreshing!"

Darren Bibby, Program Director, IDC Software Channels Research

---

"'#PARTNER tweet' provides 140 delicious spoonfuls of partnering wisdom! I recommend reading a few tweets per day to keep a healthy perspective on where to focus your business energies."

Dan Medakovic, Vice President, Operitel Corporation; President, IAMCP Canada

---

"'#PARTNER tweet' is an ingenious collection of Twitter-sized bits that accentuate the value of partnership in enhancing business opportunities."

Larry Walsh, Vice President and Group Publisher, Channel Insider

---

"The magic formula for how you become a true, trusted advisor for your customers is nicely described in '#PARTNER tweet.'"

Wolfgang Ebermann, Vice President, SMS&P EMEA, Microsoft Corporation

Dedication

To Ram, Chirag, and Neal for bringing joy and happiness every day.

Acknowledgments

Thanks to my parents and family for supporting my dreams.

Thanks to Rajesh Setty, *@UpbeatNow,* for inspiring me to think and think to do the best.

Thanks to Petri Salonen, *@PetriSalonen,* for providing great mentorship.

Thanks to Per Werngren for collaborating on partnerships throughout the years.

Thanks to Ronald Woods for trusting me to take on innovative projects.

Thanks to Bronwyn Hastings for teaching me to build long-lasting relationships.

Thanks to Jason Dirks and Jarom Reid who helped with the visual representation.

Thanks to Darren Bibby, *@darrenbibby,* for sharing his insights on partnerships.

Thanks to Chet Seligman for giving me a break in my career when I needed it most.

Thanks to Larry Walsh, *@lmwalsh2112*, for sharing his tidbits to develop this book.

Thanks to Mitchell Levy, *@HappyAbout*, and the THINKaha team for publishing this book.

Thanks to Microsoft for giving me an opportunity to serve its partner community.

Chaitra Vedullapalli, *@cvedulla*

Why Did I Write This Book?

You can only do so much alone. Your network is your accelerator for growth.

Partnerships provide you additional capacity to pursue bigger dreams.

Companies want to make the most of their partnerships but forget to strategically invest in growing them.

Your approach to partnerships will influence your partnership success.

Practice Smart Partnering and start flourishing.

Read, share, and be happy!

All the best!

Chaitra Vedullapalli, *@cvedulla*

Contents

Foreword by Dr. Petri Salonen   11

Section I
Your Partnerships   13

Section II
Your Offerings   27

Section III
Your Execution   41

Section IV
Your Service   55

Section V
Your Attitude   69

Section VI
Your People   83

Section VII
Your Community   97

About the Author   109

Foreword by Dr. Petri Salonen

Partnering is mostly misunderstood among businesspeople. Impatience for getting quick results and lack of commitment to building joint success will lead to a relationship that will not go anywhere. Partnering requires patience, and partnering is not about getting, it is about giving. With patience, partnering will lead to results and provide a platform for local, regional, or international expansion. Partnering is about building a trust between people and businesses, and without trust, there is no such thing as partnering. Trust can be built with time and trust can be torn down with one simple action. Partnering provides the most effective way for entrepreneurs to build their businesses without considerable financial commitments. In this book, Ms. Vedullapalli dives into the core of partnering, providing the keys to success.

Dr. Petri Salonen

CEO, TELLUS International Inc.

140 Bite-Sized Ideas for Succeeding in Your Partnerships

Section 1

Your Partnerships

Smart strategic partnerships can create advantages that lift you above the competition. Access to additional resources, extended reach, and enhanced market reputation are just a few of the advantages that can be gained. Learn how to make the right investments to maximize partnerships.

1

Smart Partnering will provide you an opportunity to compete against big players.

2

Smart Partnering provides insurance against your own shortcomings.

#PARTNER **tweet**

> **3**
>
> Smart Partnering provides gateways for new verticals and industries.

> **4**
>
> Smart Partnering helps you to deliver functional solutions.

5

Smart Partnering provides an opportunity to enhance your market reputation.

6

Smart Partnering provides you access to valuable resources (technology, money, and education).

7

Smart Partnering = more leads.

8

Smart Partnering has to be part of your company's DNA and not an afterthought.

9

Smart Partnering provides you the arsenal to compete on an ongoing basis.

10

Smart Partnering is a way of increasing your average deal size.

11

Smart Partnering provides a way for optimizing your marketing budget.

12

Never underestimate the initial cost of establishing partnerships.

13

Factor in the soft cost of bringing in and managing partnerships in customer engagements.

14

Have and set realistic expectations to factor in the interdependence to deliver and meet customer expectations.

140 Bite-Sized Ideas for Succeeding in Your Partnerships

15

You get a higher profitability from forging partnerships that have potential for repeat engagements.

#PARTNER **tweet**

16
Smart Partnerships provide an opportunity to turn variable costs into fixed costs.

17
Smart Partnerships provide a gateway for international expansion.

18

Smart Partnerships can help you garner more vendor attention.

19

Smart Partnerships can help you get more "qualified" leads.

20

Smart Partnerships can reduce the risk for the end customer.

140 Bite-Sized Ideas for Succeeding in Your Partnerships

Section II

Your Offerings

Make your offerings uncommonly valuable and unique and you will take first place in the marketplace. Quality is the number one secret in gaining vendor attention! And, remember, when your vendors find your offerings valuable, they will be happy to support and promote your offerings to their complete customer base.

140 Bite-Sized Ideas for Succeeding in Your Partnerships

21

You can't get paid a "premium" for "commodity" offerings.

22

How your product works is a reflection of your promise to the customers.

23

Your relationship to the customers does not end with the sale of your product. It begins there.

24

You have a "problem" if your product is not solving your customers' problems.

140 Bite-Sized Ideas for Succeeding in Your Partnerships

25

You have a "problem" if your product is creating "new problems" for your customers.

26

Too many breakdowns in using your product will create too many breakdowns in managing customer expectations.

27

Your customers are not your quality assurance department.

28

Design your offering to be part of the customer's core operating model.

29

Flexibility is not optional. Your offerings have to evolve with customer needs.

30

Customers should not only know what to expect of the product but also what to expect from the service after the purchase.

31

When it comes to quality, your products make a louder statement than your brochures.

#PARTNER **tweet**

32

Your customers don't like to solve a puzzle to find the true total cost of ownership.

33

You can cast a wider net by designing the offering to a wider audience.

34

The best way to know what your customers want from your products is to ask them.

35

Status check: do your products fit with the digital lifestyle of your customers?

36

It is your responsibility to educate and guide your customers for the next logical purchase.

37

Renewals are an expression of your customers' beliefs about the continued relevance and value of your products.

38

You can't get better "free" advertising than your customers' recommendations of your products.

39

Help customers to help themselves. [Hint: implement self-service.]

40

The better your feedback channels, the better you can listen to your customers.

140 Bite-Sized Ideas for Succeeding in Your Partnerships

Section III

Your Execution

The promise and success of your service can only become a reality through flawless execution. No company can succeed in the long run without executing on their promises of excellence. Here are some tips on how to deliver.

140 Bite-Sized Ideas for Succeeding in Your Partnerships

41

Your product is the dream. Your execution is what makes it a reality.

42

How you deliver is equally important as what you deliver.

43

Planning may be invisible, but the consequences of lack of planning become visible quickly.

44

Execution framework: design together > build together > implement together > share success together.

45

Shifting multiple deadlines = slipping in TRUST.

46

Win the DEAL and you can CELEBRATE; win in the EXECUTION and let the customer CELEBRATE.

#PARTNER **tweet**

> **47**
>
> The sale is the start of the relationship, and the execution is the ongoing relationship.

> **48**
>
> Get the execution right and you get the right to sell again.

49

Plan for quick wins to ensure continued customer engagement.

50

Execution excellence is NOT a one-time game.

51

A good product and a bad implementation are sure to result in a bad customer experience.

52

The three Cs of execution = clarity, competence, and collaboration.

53

Having the right people in the right place lays the foundation for flawless execution.

54

Good project governance provides the necessary insurance policy for good execution.

55

Creating and monitoring compelling scorecards provide the necessary reality checks required for flawless execution.

56

Your ability to execute well may provide you the biggest competitive advantage in the marketplace.

57

Executing successfully will require regular re-prioritization.

58

No discipline = no execution.

59

The higher the complexity of the project, the greater the need for good processes.

#PARTNER **tweet**

60

Building the capacity to execute well in the future is equally important as executing well now.

140 Bite-Sized Ideas for Succeeding in Your Partnerships

Section IV

Your Service

Your client service is equally as important as your product. While it's easy to focus your customer service efforts on obvious touch points, like call centers, clients experience your service across all of the interactions they have with your product—from human (sales, marketing, finance, etc.) to digital (website, email, newsletters, etc.). It's important to make every customer interaction a valuable experience.

61

Your customers expect superior service at EVERY touch point.

62

Different customers value different things. Customize your relationship and service experience.

63

Continue to add value by knowing what the customer perceives as valuable.

64

Superior service can transform satisfied customers to loyal customers.

65

Service is where you establish an emotional connection with your customer.

66

Identify and measure what really matters (KPIs and customer feedback).

#PARTNER **tweet**

67

Learn to notice subtle shifts in customer language to predict service experience and satisfaction.

68

Service leadership is MANDATORY to gain customer loyalty.

69

Benchmark against the best inside and outside your industry.

70

No customer complains about relevant timely communication.

71

People may not notice good service but they surely will notice lack of good service.

72

Excellent customer service = happy customers = new referrals = new revenue.

73

Bad customer service provides a ticket to losing a good customer.

#PARTNER **tweet**

74

Customers go to places where they feel welcomed, valued, and comfortable.

75

Customer service spans way beyond your interactions through the call center.

76

Urgency, empathy, and care to solve your customers' problems will go a long way.

#PARTNER **tweet**

77

Have a good recovery plan for service breakdowns.

78

Proactively engaging with your customers is a quick way to gain their mindshare.

79

Excellent customer service = increased loyalty = higher profits.

80

The key to excellent customer service is to know your company, your offering, and your customers.

140 Bite-Sized Ideas for Succeeding in Your Partnerships

Section V

Your Attitude

The secret to success is to truly care about making a difference to your customers and partners. Your attitude is reflected in your daily actions and your clients will know immediately when your attitude is not sincere.

81

You can't expect superior returns by producing mediocre results.

82

Cooperate and coordinate with your customers so that they can compete in the marketplace.

83

Breaking trust is simple: you over-promise and under-deliver.

84

Credibility might win you a deal. Credibility and caring will win you a relationship.

85

You may be focusing on putting in the hours, but the customer is focusing on the value you pack into those hours.

86

You can't build a long-term relationship in the short term.

87

Your internal culture is reflected in your external interactions with your customers.

88

Being easy to work with is a BASIC expectation from your customers.

89

Professionalism is not only required to win new relationships but also to maintain and grow relationships in the long run.

90

The better your solution fits in the customer's "big picture" the more influence you have on the deal.

91

You don't win prizes for finding the best excuses for not producing results.

92

You make the choice: If you listen, you can respond. If you don't listen, you will react.

93

You can shy away from your responsibilities, but you can't escape the consequences of your actions.

94

Remember to walk the extra mile of bringing innovation to bring out the best in your customers.

95

If you don't have pride in your work, how can you make your customers proud of your work?

96

Whether you touch a customer directly or not, you have the responsibility to delight them.

97

Reliability is NOT optional.

98

You can change and adapt voluntarily or wait for the marketplace to force you to change and adapt.

99

Make every customer interaction a learning experience.

100

Don't expect brownie points for adding extra complexity in your customers' lives.

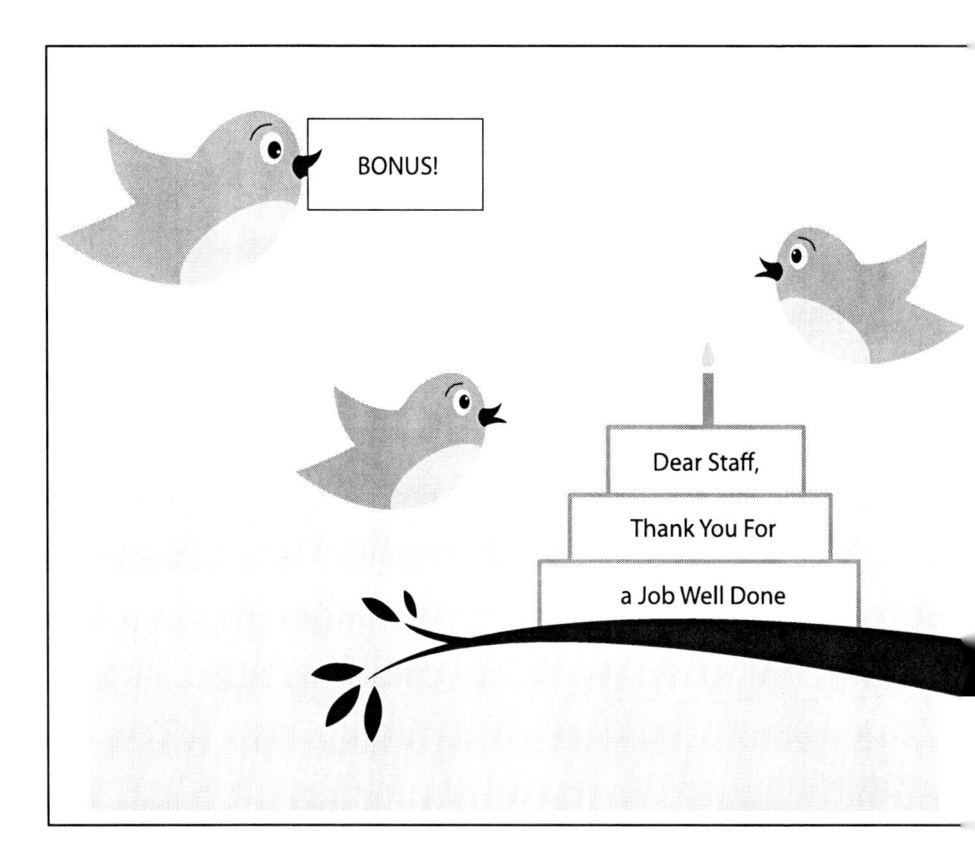

140 Bite-Sized Ideas for Succeeding in Your Partnerships

BONUS!

Dear Staff,

Thank You For

a Job Well Done

Section VI

Your People

Your people are your biggest asset. They make the promises in the marketplace, fulfill those promises to your clients, and provide the excellent customer service that is critical to your product's or offering's success. Care for your people and create a culture where they value caring for your customers and partners.

140 Bite-Sized Ideas for Succeeding in Your Partnerships

101

Your promises are ONLY as good as the people who will deliver on them.

102

Your people are your brand ambassadors.

103

If you don't care for your people, don't expect them to care for your customers.

104

If you direct, your people may comply. If you inspire, people will excel.

105

Winning people create winning teams. Winning teams create winning cultures. Winning cultures create winning companies.

#PARTNER **tweet**

106

Creating a world-class service requires an investment in world-class education for your people.

107

There is a world of difference between "walking the talk" and "talking the talk."

108

Confusion in culture is created by people who are not aligned with your vision and values.

109

Unhappy employees rarely create happy customers.

110

Strive to create alignment with ALL the people who support your business (including vendors, partners, etc.).

111

Invest in educating your people on a common service language that is powerful and inspiring.

#PARTNER **tweet**

112

If your people are not operating on their strengths, they will be frustrated and also make your customers frustrated.

113

Design your incentives to encourage people to collaborate and win as teams.

114

Nobody complains about an overdose of good compliments.

115

Teach your people to ALWAYS see the big picture from the customer's point of view.

116

Good orientation of new employees is not a cost. It's an investment for the future.

117

Inspire your people to become corporate citizens inside and outside.

118

Design a mentorship program to create new possibilities for growth of your people.

119

Strive to get the mindshare of your people and not their physical presence.

120

Train your people NOT to make commitments they cannot fulfill.

140 Bite-Sized Ideas for Succeeding in Your Partnerships

Section VII

Your Community

The communities that you belong to will provide you with your best opportunities for growth and change.

140 Bite-Sized Ideas for Succeeding in Your Partnerships

121

Take time to create a place for your customers to interact with each other.

122

Actively listen to conversations in the community to gain insights.

123

Proactively participating and adding value to the community is a quick way to showcase thought leadership.

124

Providing valuable help in the community has a direct influence on your brand.

125

Used well, your community can be a powerful demand-generation engine.

126

Your people have an opportunity to build powerful personal brands through the community.

127

To succeed in a network, think like a node.

128

Rather than advertising, participate in the community to build and grow relationships.

129

Volunteer to help with community activities to increase your visibility.

130

Leverage your community to influence best practices for the benefit of all.

#PARTNER **tweet**

131

Analytics from the community helps you to understand why they are doing what they are doing.

132

Community > Conversations > Credibility > Demand

133

Community provides a window into people's passions.

134
Conversations among people are more important than marketing messages directed at them.

135
Real conversations in communities provide honest, reliable sources of opinion.

136

In the new world, communities provide a powerful platform for ongoing research.

137

Communities provide a platform for identifying and influencing the influencers.

138

Understanding the motivations via listening to conversations can help you redesign your offers to the marketplace.

139

Community conversations provide insights and early warnings on key issues.

140

Community helps you to distribute and consume relevant content.

About the Author

Chaitra Vedullapalli is the Senior Director of WW Sales and Marketing Communications, where she oversees the information workplace for Microsoft Sales Force.

Past work includes shaping the Microsoft Customer and Partner Self Service Experience that touched over 10 million customers and 1 million partners. She was also an integral part of creating the Service Culture at Microsoft and an architect of the Microsoft-IAMCP (International Association of Microsoft Certified Partners) innovation program.

Chaitra Vedullapalli has also served as Director of Licensing and PartnerNetwork at Oracle where her projects drove licensing simplification and enabled state-of-the-art innovations in Partner Self Service Experience.

Chaitra Vedullapalli holds a Patent in WebMethods and Bachelor's of Electrical Engineering from RVCE, Bangalore, and is currently active in community efforts to help children in need.